The A.I.R. Effect

31 Laws to Lead With Identity, Strategy,
and Spiritual Intelligence

Dr. Ansonya L. Burke

Contents

Introduction

Leadership is not reserved for those with titles, platforms, or public recognition. It is a divine invitation—extended to all. Whether you're running a business, raising a family, teaching a classroom, launching a ministry, or simply navigating the complexities of life, **you are a leader**. You were designed to lead, and your first assignment is not others—but yourself.

True leadership begins with **self-government**. Before you cast vision or carry others, you first have to take a concious look in the mirror. Leadership demands that you develop self-discipline, cultivate inner clarity, and build the kind of mindset that can weather pressure without collapsing. When you lead yourself with intention, others will begin to rise around you. Not because you demanded it—but because you embodied it.

This book offers you more than leadership theory. It offers a **transformational framework** rooted in identity, strategy, and spiritual intelligence. It introduces **The A.I .R. Effect**—a divine, spirit-led approach to personal and leadership growth.

Activate your identity: Own who you are, reclaim your voice, and align with your God-given authority.

Impart wisdom and strength to others: Lead from overflow, communicate with prophetic clarity, and build culture with integrity.

Release legacy: Raise others, multiply impact, and lead with a rhythm of rest, purpose, and divine precision.

These three phases—**Activate. Impart. Release.**—form the A.I.R. Framework, and they are your path to becoming a leader marked by wholeness, clarity, and supernatural strength.

This journey is deeply connected to the principles first introduced in *Eikonic Leadership: 8 Qualities That Separate You from the Ordinary*. That book was a foundational work, helping leaders identify the internal markers of distinction. *The A.I.R. Effect* builds upon that legacy—offering **31 powerful leadership laws** that take you deeper into your calling, your character, and your capacity to influence and uplift others.

You won't find gimmicks here. You'll find **biblical truth**, personal wisdom, and a system that honors both **the process and your humanity** as an evolving leader.

Whether you're in the pulpit or behind the scenes, in a boardroom or at your kitchen table—this book will meet you where you are and stretch you into who you're becoming.

If you've ever felt like leadership was meant for someone "more qualified," **this is your reminder that leadership begins with you**. That what you cultivate privately is what will overflow publicly. That what you refine in the secret place is what will shape others in the open.

So breathe deeply. Step boldly. And allow The A.I.R. Effect to ignite the leader within. Let's get to work!

SECTION I: ACTIVATE

PRINCIPLE THEMES:
Identity, Self-Awareness, Inner Alignment

Focus Keys:
Internal mastery, healing, clarity, mindset, personal growth

Principle 1

The Law of Empowerment

LEADERS ARE OFTEN SEEN as visionaries, but there is a common misconception that people will follow a leader simply because of the vision they cast. This is far from reality. People must first believe in *you* before they can fully embrace the vision you are presenting. This is the principle of empowerment. You empower others not through eloquent speeches or grand ideas but through the value you bring as a person—your authenticity, character, and ability to connect with others on a meaningful level.

Empowerment Starts with You

Every leader must ask themselves: *Who am I, and what makes me empowering?* Leadership begins with self-awareness. Your unique experiences, lessons learned, and personal growth are tools that can empower others to grow and succeed. Whether you're leading a church congregation, managing a team in the workplace, or mentoring students in education, your ability to empower others comes from your willingness to share your journey and invest in their potential.

For example:

- In ministry, sharing how you overcame personal struggles can inspire someone to trust God through their own challenges.

- In the marketplace, being transparent about failures can encourage your team to take risks without fear of judgment.

- In education, showing vulnerability about your own learning process can motivate students to persevere through difficulties.

Empowerment is not about perfection but about connection. When people see that you are invested in their growth and believe in their potential, they will be more willing to follow your leadership.

Becoming a Beacon of Direction

Leadership can sometimes feel isolating. You may wonder if your efforts are making a difference or if anyone notices the sacrifices you make. However, leadership is not about recognition—it's about being a beacon of direction for those who look to you for guidance.

To be this beacon:

- Focus on personal growth—spiritually, emotionally, and intellectually—so you can lead from a place of strength and clarity.

- Be consistent in your actions and values; people need leaders they can trust.

- Offer encouragement and clarity when others feel lost or uncertain.

For instance:

- A pastor might guide their congregation by modeling faith during difficult times.

- A business leader might provide clear direction during periods of uncertainty or change.

- A teacher might help students navigate challenges

by offering tools for problem-solving rather than just answers.

Being a beacon doesn't mean having all the answers—it means being present, steady, and committed to helping others find their way.

The Process Over the Destination

In our results-driven culture, it's easy to become fixated on achieving goals and reaching milestones. However, true empowerment happens during the process—not just at the destination. Leaders who focus solely on outcomes miss the opportunity to teach others how to grow through challenges and setbacks.

For example:

- In ministry: Encourage congregants to embrace spiritual growth as an ongoing journey rather than expecting instant transformation.

- In business: Celebrate small wins with your team to reinforce the value of progress over perfection.

- In education: Help students see how their daily efforts contribute to long-term success rather than focusing only on final grades or test scores.

By embracing the process yourself and modeling this mindset for others, you empower them to appreciate their own journey and find meaning in every step along the way.

Courage Fuels Confidence

Many people believe they need confidence before stepping into leadership roles or pursuing big dreams. However, confidence often follows courage—it doesn't precede it. Taking bold steps despite fear or uncertainty is what builds confidence over time.

This principle applies across all areas of leadership:

- In ministry: Starting a new initiative or outreach program may feel daunting at first, but stepping out in faith inspires others to do the same.

- In business: Pitching an innovative idea or challenging the status quo requires courage but can lead to breakthroughs for your team or organization.

- In education: Trying new teaching methods or addressing difficult topics with students takes bravery but can create lasting impact in their lives.

As you take courageous steps forward—even when insecurities arise—you model resilience for those around you. This kind of leadership empowers others to face their fears and pursue their potential with boldness.

The Gift of Rest

In today's hustle culture, rest is often undervalued or seen as unproductive. Yet great leaders understand that rest is essential for sustained empowerment. When you prioritize rest and renewal, you lead from a place of abundance rather than burnout—and this allows you to pour into others more effectively.

Consider these applications:

- In ministry: Prioritize Sabbath rest as an act of obedience and renewal for yourself and your team. Show your congregation that rest is part of God's design for human flourishing.

- In business: Model work-life balance by setting boundaries and encouraging employees to recharge without guilt.

- In education: Take moments to pause and reflect so that you can bring fresh energy and creativity into your teaching.

- In life: Protect your time to reflect and recharge.

Rest isn't just about physical recovery—it's about creating space for reflection, inspiration, and spiritual renewal so that you can continue empowering others with clarity and purpose.

Declaration and Affirmation

As leaders in ministry, marketplace, or education, it's important to speak life over yourself regularly. Let this declaration serve as both encouragement and reminder:

> *I will lead wisely and empower those around me toward purpose-filled lives.*
> *I am valuable because of who I am—not just what I do.*
> *I am a beacon of direction for those seeking guidance.*
> *I will embrace each step of my journey while helping others do the same.*
> *I am destined to make an impact—one life at a time.*

Principle 2

The Law of Identifying Growth Edges

EVERY LEADER MUST DEVELOP the ability to identify both their own strengths and growth edges, as well as those of the people they lead. This awareness is essential for cultivating effective teams, fostering personal development, and achieving collective goals. Leaders who embrace this principle empower others to thrive by helping them recognize their potential and navigate their areas for improvement.

Leaders as Path Pavers

Leaders are not just managers or decision-makers—they are path pavers who guide others toward self-awareness and growth. A great leader helps individuals identify their unique talents and growth edges, teaching them how to leverage their strengths while seeking support in areas where they may lack expertise or confidence.

For example:

- In ministry: A pastor may encourage someone with a gift for hospitality to lead a welcoming team while mentoring someone struggling with public speaking to develop their communication skills.

- In the marketplace: A manager might assign a creative thinker to spearhead brainstorming sessions while pairing them with an analytical colleague to handle execution details.

- In education: A teacher might recognize a student's talent for leadership but help them work on collaboration skills to better function in group settings.

Effective leaders understand that success is not about individual glory but about fostering collaboration and ensuring the right people are in the right roles. They prioritize the mission over personal recognition, paving the way for others to shine.

Growth Edges as Opportunities

It's easy to view growth edges (or weaknesses) as setbacks or failures, but exceptional leaders see them as opportunities. These areas of limitation create space for collaboration, humility, and reliance on God's strength. They remind us that leadership isn't about doing everything perfectly—it's about doing what we can while inviting others into the process.

For instance:

- In ministry: A leader might admit they struggle with administrative tasks and delegate those responsibilities to someone gifted in organization, allowing them to focus on teaching or pastoral care.

- In business: A CEO might acknowledge that they're not skilled in digital marketing and hire an expert to lead that area of the company.

- In education: A principal might recognize that they need support in curriculum design and partner with experienced teachers to create effective programs.

When leaders embrace their growth edges, they model vulnerability and authenticity, creating an environment where others feel safe to do the same.

Shifting Perspective in Difficult Seasons

Every leader will face seasons where their growth edges feel overwhelming—times when insecurity, doubt, or exhaustion threaten to derail progress. Exceptional leaders understand that these moments require a shift in perspective. Instead of dwelling on what they *cannot* do, they focus on what they *can* do and what is within their control.

For example:

- A ministry leader facing criticism might focus on deepening their prayer life and seeking wise counsel rather than trying to please everyone.

- A business leader struggling with declining sales might focus on improving customer relationships rather than obsessing over immediate profits.

- An educator feeling burned out might focus on small victories in the classroom rather than striving for perfection every day.

By reframing limitations as opportunities for growth and problem-solving, leaders inspire resilience in themselves and those they lead.

The Limits of Leadership

One of the hardest lessons for leaders to learn is that no matter how much effort they invest in teaching, mentoring, or inspiring someone, they cannot control the outcome. People must ultimately take responsibility for their own actions and choices.

For example:

- In ministry: A pastor may pour time into counseling someone who ultimately chooses not to change destructive behavior.

- In business: A manager may mentor an employee who decides not to apply learned skills or pursue growth opportunities.

- In education: A teacher may work tirelessly with a student who refuses to engage or put in effort.

Exceptional leaders recognize that their role is not to force results but to plant seeds of growth and offer guidance.

They release themselves from the burden of outcomes while remaining faithful in their efforts.

Declaration and Affirmation

As leaders across ministry, marketplace, and education, we must embrace our own growth edges while helping others navigate theirs. Let this declaration serve as both encouragement and commitment:

> *I declare that I will embrace my growth edges as opportunities for connection, collaboration, and reliance on God's strength.*
>
> *I will lead with wisdom and humility, guiding others toward self-awareness and equipping them with tools for success.*
>
> *I will release control over outcomes while remaining faithful in my efforts to empower those I lead.*

Principle 3

The Law of Wholeness Over Hustle

LEADERSHIP BEGINS WITH KNOWING where you are going. You cannot lead others effectively if you lack clarity about your destination or the path to get there. Visionary leaders are intentional about defining their goals, aligning their motives, and navigating challenges with courage and purpose. They inspire others by casting a clear vision while embracing the journey along the way.

Navigating Challenges: Courage in Tumultuous Waters

Life and leadership are rarely smooth sailing. Obstacles will arise, and storms will test your resolve. The question is: *How do you respond when challenges come?* Great leaders don't freeze at the sight of complications—they become problem solvers who focus on finding resolutions with courage and creativity.

For example:

- In ministry: A pastor facing dwindling attendance might prayerfully seek innovative ways to engage the community rather than succumbing to discouragement.

- In business: A manager dealing with unexpected setbacks on a project might rally their team to brainstorm solutions instead of assigning blame.

- In education: A teacher encountering resistance from students might adapt their teaching methods to meet them where they are.

Visionary leaders embrace challenges as opportunities for growth, modeling resilience for those they lead.

Clarity: Defining Your Destination

You cannot lead others effectively without first gaining clarity about your own goals and objectives. Visionary leaders take time to reflect, pray, and plan so they can articulate a clear path forward. This clarity not only guides their own actions but also inspires confidence in those who follow them.

For instance:

- In ministry: A church leader might define their vision for outreach by setting specific goals, such as feeding a certain number of families or launching a new discipleship program.

- In business: A CEO might break down a long-term goal into quarterly milestones that keep the team focused and motivated.

- In education: A principal might set clear objectives for improving student performance while outlining actionable steps for teachers to implement.

Clarity creates momentum. It allows leaders to move forward with confidence while empowering others to do the same.

Intentionality: Aligning Motives with Purpose

Our intentions shape our leadership. Visionary leaders regularly examine their motives, asking themselves whether their actions are guided by selflessness or selfishness. True leadership is not about personal gain—it's about serving others and advancing a greater purpose.

For example:

- In ministry: A pastor might evaluate whether their decisions are motivated by a desire to glorify God or by personal recognition.

- In business: A manager might prioritize what's best for the team rather than making choices that solely benefit their own career advancement.

- In education: A teacher might focus on what's best for students' long-term growth rather than simply aiming for higher test scores.

Selfless leaders inspire trust and loyalty because they put others before themselves, creating environments where people feel valued and supported.

Embracing the Journey: Focusing on the Process

While it's important to have a clear destination in mind, visionary leaders understand that the process is just as valuable as the outcome. They encourage others to embrace each step of the journey, cultivating gratitude for present moments rather than fixating solely on future achievements.

For instance:

- In ministry: A leader might remind their congregation that spiritual growth happens over time and encourage them to celebrate small victories in faith.

- In business: A manager might recognize team members' progress during a challenging project rather than waiting until completion to offer praise.

- In education: A teacher might help students reflect on how much they've learned throughout a semester rather than focusing only on final grades.

By focusing on the process, leaders model an attitude of gratitude and perseverance that inspires others to stay engaged in their own journeys.

Declaration and Affirmation

I declare pure intentions and selflessness in my heart as I lead others toward meaningful and fulfilling destinations in their lives.

I commit to leading with integrity, honesty, and loyalty to those who trust me.

I will embrace both the process and the destination, living each moment with gratitude while inspiring others to do the same.

Principle 4

The Law of Visionary Leadership

LEADERSHIP IS AN INVESTMENT that yields exponential benefits over time. The more intentional you are about leading and developing others, the more growth you will see in yourself and those you serve. This principle reflects the timeless truth of sowing and reaping: those who sow with care and purpose will eventually reap a meaningful harvest.

The Sower: Planting Seeds of Growth

As a leader, you are a sower—someone who plants seeds of wisdom, encouragement, and guidance in the lives of others. Every conversation, every moment of mentorship, and every act of service is an opportunity to sow seeds that will one day bear fruit.

For example:

- In ministry: A pastor might invest time teaching a young leader how to preach or lead small groups, knowing that their influence will multiply as that leader grows.

- In the marketplace: A manager might mentor an employee on leadership skills, planting seeds for their future success as a team leader or executive.

- In education: A teacher might encourage a struggling student by helping them see their potential, planting seeds of confidence and perseverance.

The key is to focus on what you are giving rather than what you are gaining. Exceptional leaders understand that their role is to empower others by planting seeds that may take years to grow but will ultimately make a lasting impact.

The Harvest: Growing Through the Process

Harvesting isn't about how much you gain from others—it's about how much *you* grow in the process of sowing. Exceptional leaders prioritize their own personal and spiritual growth as they invest in others. The greatest harvest comes not from external accolades but from internal development—gaining wisdom, discernment, and deeper self-awareness.

For instance:

- In ministry: A leader who invests in mentoring others may find themselves growing in patience, humility, and spiritual maturity.

- In business: A manager who empowers their team may develop stronger communication skills and a greater capacity for collaboration.

- In education: A teacher who pours into students may discover new teaching strategies or gain fresh insights into how people learn.

Growth is reciprocal; as you help others grow, you grow alongside them. This mindset shifts leadership from being transactional to transformational.

The Waiting Period: Cultivating Patience

One of the most challenging aspects of leadership is the waiting period between sowing and reaping. You can control when you plant seeds by investing time and energy into others, but you cannot control when—or if—those seeds will bear fruit. This waiting period requires patience, diligence, and trust in the process.

During this time:

- In ministry: A pastor might feel discouraged when their congregation doesn't immediately respond to a new initiative but must trust that God is working behind the scenes.

- In business: A manager might feel frustrated when an employee doesn't show immediate improvement after coaching but must remain committed to their development.

- In education: A teacher might feel disheartened when students don't grasp a concept right away but must continue teaching with hope and persistence.

The waiting period builds character by teaching leaders to let go of control and focus on what they *can* do—modeling patience, resilience, and faith for those they lead.

Seasons of Sowing and Reaping

Leadership requires recognizing the seasons in your life—times for pouring into others and times for nurturing yourself. There are seasons to plant seeds by investing in others' growth, but there are also seasons to step back, recharge, and tend to your own personal and spiritual needs.

For example:

- In ministry: A leader might dedicate one season to discipling others through small groups while taking another season to deepen their own relationship with God through prayer and study.

- In business: A manager might spend one season focused on mentoring employees while using another season for professional development or strategic planning.

- In education: A teacher might spend one semester heavily involved in extracurricular activities while taking another semester to focus on self-care or pursuing advanced training.

Recognizing these seasons prevents burnout and ensures that you can continue leading effectively over the long term. Leaders who nurture themselves are better equipped to nurture others.

Declaration and Affirmation

As leaders across ministry, marketplace, and education, we must commit ourselves to sowing seeds of growth while embracing patience during the waiting periods. Let this declaration guide your heart:

I declare that I will faithfully plant seeds of wisdom, encouragement, and empowerment in the lives of those I lead without seeking personal gain or using manipulation tactics.

I am a conscious leader who nurtures both myself and others with intention and care.

I will embrace the seasons of sowing and reaping with patience, trusting that growth happens in its own time.

Principle 5

The Law of Value Creation

Leadership is about serving others and creating value in their lives. When you give your time, energy, and wisdom to those you lead, you build trust, foster respect, and strengthen relationships. People are more likely to follow your guidance when they know you genuinely care about their well-being. Leaders who serve wholeheartedly inspire loyalty and transformation in the lives of others.

Defining Your Sphere: Who Are You Leading?

To create value as a leader, you must first identify your target audience. Who are you called to lead? Your experiences, challenges, and victories equip you to inspire and guide those who are navigating similar trials. By understanding who your audience is, you can tailor your leadership to meet their unique needs.

For example:

- In ministry: A pastor might focus on mentoring young leaders who are passionate about serving but lack direction.

- In business: A manager might identify employees who need professional development and create opportunities for their growth.

- In education: A teacher might recognize students struggling with self-confidence and provide encouragement to help them succeed.

Speak your truth authentically and give the best of yourself to those you are leading. When you know your audience, you can lead with greater impact.

Discovering Your Internal Assets: What Makes You Valuable?

Every leader has unique gifts, skills, and experiences that make them valuable to others. Take time to reflect on what you have to offer. Your knowledge, wisdom, and ability to empathize are powerful tools that can transform lives.

For instance:

- In ministry: A leader might draw from personal struggles with faith to encourage someone going through a season of doubt.

- In business: A manager might use their expertise in problem-solving to mentor employees facing challenges in their roles.

- In education: A teacher might share their passion for learning to inspire students to pursue their own interests.

Ask yourself: *How can I improve someone else's life today?* The value inside you is meant to be shared.

Empathy in Action: Becoming a Valuable Leader

To truly create value in others' lives, leaders must lead with empathy. Empathy involves understanding the needs, struggles, and aspirations of those you serve. When people feel seen and heard, they are more likely to trust your leadership.

For example:

- In ministry: A pastor might listen attentively to

a congregant's concerns without rushing to offer solutions, showing genuine care for their journey.

- In business: A manager might take time to understand an employee's career goals and offer guidance on how they can achieve them.

- In education: A teacher might adapt lessons for a student who learns differently, demonstrating a commitment to their success.

Empathy transforms leadership from transactional to relational. By valuing people's experiences and perspectives, you become a leader worth following.

The Impact of Adding Value

Why should leaders focus on adding value? Because leadership is ultimately about making a difference in the lives of others. When you serve people well—helping them grow, heal, or achieve success—you contribute to their transformation. Witnessing this growth brings fulfillment and gratitude that fuels your own leadership journey.

For example:

- In ministry: Seeing someone deepen their faith because of your mentorship reinforces your calling as a spiritual leader.

- In business: Watching an employee excel after implementing your advice affirms the importance of investing in others' development.

- In education: Seeing a student overcome obstacles and thrive because of your encouragement reminds you why teaching matters.

Adding value isn't just about what you give—it's about the legacy you leave behind in the lives of others.

Declaration and Affirmation

I declare that I am becoming a valuable leader who creates meaningful impact in the lives of those I serve. I will lead with empathy, care deeply about others' needs, and commit myself to helping them grow into their best selves.

Principle 6

The Law of Foundational Trust

TRUST IS THE CORNERSTONE of effective leadership. Without trust, relationships falter, teams crumble, and visions fail to take root. A leader who builds trust creates a solid foundation upon which others can grow, collaborate, and succeed. Trustworthy leaders inspire loyalty, respect, and confidence in those they serve.

Trust as the Foundation of Leadership

Leadership without trust is like building a house on sand—it cannot withstand the storms of life. Trust is the bedrock upon which all successful relationships and organizations are built. Leaders must prioritize cultivating trust through their actions, words, and decisions.

For example:

- In ministry: A pastor who consistently shows compassion and integrity earns the trust of their congregation, fostering unity within the church.

- In business: A manager who follows through on promises builds credibility with their team, creating a culture of accountability.

- In education: A teacher who listens to students' concerns with empathy gains their respect, making the classroom a safe space for learning.

Trustworthy leaders create environments where people feel secure and valued.

Honest Decisions: Leading with Integrity

Trust is built when leaders make decisions rooted in honesty and fairness. This means prioritizing loyalty to others over personal gain. Leaders who consistently act with integrity earn the respect of those they lead.

For instance:

- In ministry: A leader might address conflicts within their team transparently, ensuring that de-

cisions are made in the best interest of everyone
involved.

- In business: A CEO might turn down a lucrative
  deal that compromises company values or employee well-being.

- In education: A principal might advocate for
  policies that benefit students and teachers rather
  than succumbing to external pressures.

Honest decisions demonstrate that leaders value people
over profit or power.

Shunning Shortcuts: Prioritizing Excellence

Great leaders avoid shortcuts because they understand
that lasting success requires diligence and quality. While
quick fixes may offer temporary relief, they often under-
mine long-term results. Leaders who focus on excellence
inspire others to do the same.

For example:

- In ministry: A pastor might take time to prepare
  meaningful sermons rather than rushing through
  preparation for convenience.

- In business: A manager might encourage their team to prioritize quality over speed in delivering projects, even if it means adjusting deadlines.

- In education: A teacher might invest extra time in lesson planning to ensure students fully grasp concepts rather than rushing through material.

Leaders who value excellence build trust by showing they care about doing things the right way.

Lasting Leadership: Earning Respect

Trustworthy leadership isn't built overnight—it's earned through consistency, humility, and sound decision-making. Leaders who admit their mistakes and learn from them gain respect that endures beyond temporary successes.

For instance:

- In ministry: A leader who apologizes for missteps models humility and fosters reconciliation within their community.

- In business: A manager who takes responsibility for a failed initiative earns credibility with their team by demonstrating accountability.

- In education: A teacher who acknowledges errors in grading or instruction builds trust with students by showing fairness.

Lasting leadership is grounded in respect earned through authenticity and reliability.

Declaration and Affirmation

I declare that I am a trusted leader who values people and builds relationships on a foundation of integrity and care.

I commit to establishing trust through honest decisions, excellence, and humility as I lead others toward lasting success.

Principle 7

The Law of Internal Mastery

PEOPLE ARE DRAWN TO leaders who demonstrate strength, courage, and results. Admirable achievement isn't about boasting—it's about showing others what is possible through diligence, resilience, and loyalty. Leaders inspire others by overcoming obstacles with grace and achieving success that benefits not just themselves but those they lead.

The Admiration Factor: Why People Follow You

People follow leaders they admire—those who embody qualities like integrity, strength, and perseverance. Respect is at the heart of admiration; when people respect you as a leader, they are more likely to follow your guidance.

For example:

- In ministry: Congregants admire pastors who live out their faith authentically and lead by example in both word and deed.

- In business: Employees respect managers who treat them fairly while maintaining high standards for performance.

- In education: Students look up to teachers who demonstrate passion for learning while showing genuine care for their success.

Leaders earn admiration by consistently modeling the values they expect from others.

Courage: The Boldness to Lead

Courage is an essential quality for any leader. People admire those who step up in difficult situations, take risks for what is right, and persevere against all odds. Courageous leaders inspire others to face challenges with confidence.

For instance:

- In ministry: A pastor might boldly address injustice within their community despite potential backlash because it aligns with biblical principles.

- In business: A CEO might take calculated risks to innovate despite uncertainty in the market, inspiring employees to think creatively.

- In education: A teacher might advocate for students' needs even when it requires challenging outdated policies or practices.

Courageous leaders show others what it means to lead with conviction and fearlessness.

Results That Inspire Confidence

Success attracts followers because it demonstrates competence and determination. People are drawn to leaders with a track record of accomplishments—not because they boast about results but because they model what's possible through hard work.

For example:

- In ministry: A leader whose outreach programs have transformed lives inspires others to join in their mission.

- In business: A manager whose team consistently meets or exceeds goals motivates employees to strive for excellence.

- In education: A teacher whose students achieve significant growth inspires colleagues to adopt similar strategies.

Results matter because they build confidence in your ability to lead effectively.

Earning Respect Through Loyalty

Respect is not given—it's earned through loyalty and commitment to those you serve. Leaders who remain steadfast in an ever-changing world demonstrate reliability that inspires trust and admiration.

For instance:

- In ministry: A pastor who remains faithful during difficult seasons shows congregants what it means to persevere in faith.

- In business: A manager who prioritizes employee well-being during organizational changes demonstrates loyalty that earns long-term respect.

- In education: A teacher who invests time in struggling students shows commitment that inspires gratitude from both students and parents.

Loyalty is an asset that strengthens relationships between leaders and those they serve.

Declaration and Affirmation

I declare that I am committed to achieving great things not for my own glory but to inspire others toward success. I am an overcomer whose courage, loyalty, and results create lasting impact for those I lead.

Principle 8

The Law of Objective Evaluation

EFFECTIVE LEADERS POSSESS THE ability to evaluate situations, people, and outcomes through an objective lens. They balance intuition with logic, personal perspective with fairness, and short-term decisions with long-term vision. Leaders who master objective evaluation make sound decisions that inspire confidence and drive success.

Intuition: Trusting Your Strengths

Every leader has intuition, but not all intuition is created equal. People tend to be intuitive in areas where they are naturally gifted or experienced. Great leaders learn to trust their God-given instincts in their areas of strength while remaining objective when navigating unfamiliar territory.

For example:

- In ministry: A pastor may intuitively sense when someone in their congregation is struggling emotionally and respond with compassion.

- In business: A manager may instinctively know how to motivate their team during a challenging project but seek input when making technical decisions outside their expertise.

- In education: A teacher may intuitively adapt lessons to meet students' needs while consulting colleagues for strategies in areas they feel less confident.

Leaders must flow in their strengths while seeking wisdom and objectivity in areas where they lack expertise.

Read and React: Staying Ready to Respond

Great leaders develop a "read-and-react" instinct—they are constantly evaluating situations and preparing to respond effectively. This requires staying alert, thinking critically, and being adaptable in the face of unexpected challenges.

For instance:

- In ministry: A leader might adjust a sermon mid-delivery based on the congregation's response, ensuring the message resonates deeply.

- In business: A manager might pivot a project's direction after identifying inefficiencies during its early stages.

- In education: A teacher might modify a lesson plan on the spot if students are struggling to grasp a concept.

Leaders who can read situations quickly and react thoughtfully inspire trust and confidence in those they lead.

Identity Lens: Seeing Beyond Yourself

Who you are shapes how you see the world. Your thoughts, feelings, and experiences influence how you evaluate situations. To lead with excellence, leaders must learn to step outside themselves—setting aside personal biases to make fair and objective decisions.

For example:

- In ministry: A pastor might set aside personal preferences when choosing worship styles that best serve the congregation as a whole.

- In business: A manager might evaluate employee performance based on measurable results rather than personal opinions or relationships.

- In education: A teacher might approach student behavior with empathy rather than judgment, considering external factors that could be influencing it.

Objective leaders cultivate self-awareness, ensuring their decisions reflect fairness rather than personal bias.

Perceivers: Planning for the Future

Visionary leaders see beyond the present moment—they anticipate trends, foresee challenges, and plan for long-term success. This ability to "see ahead" allows them to position themselves and their teams for sustainable growth.

For instance:

- In ministry: A church leader might plan outreach programs that address emerging community needs before they become critical issues.

- In business: A CEO might invest in new technologies that align with future market trends, ensuring the company remains competitive.

- In education: An administrator might implement policies that prepare students for careers in industries that are rapidly evolving.

Leaders who take a broad view of situations inspire confidence by demonstrating foresight and strategic thinking.

Declaration and Affirmation

> *I declare that I am developing my ability to evaluate situations objectively, balancing intuition with wisdom and fairness.*
>
> *I am a leader who plans with vision, evaluates with clarity, and responds with confidence for long-term success.*

Principle 9

The Law of Forward Motion

MOMENTUM IS THE LIFEBLOOD of progress. People feel most inspired, motivated, and productive when they sense forward motion in an organization or team. Leaders who create momentum cultivate an atmosphere of belief, energy, and advancement that drives success and inspires action.

Motivation Through Momentum

Momentum creates motivation. When people see progress—when they feel that things are moving forward—they are inspired to work harder, stay engaged, and remain hopeful about future opportunities. Momentum generates belief in advancement and fosters a culture of productivity.

For example:

- In ministry: A pastor who celebrates small wins in church growth or outreach inspires the congregation to stay committed to the vision.

- In business: A manager who highlights incremental achievements during a project motivates employees to keep striving toward the end goal.

- In education: A teacher who recognizes students' progress throughout a semester encourages them to stay focused on their learning journey.

Leaders who build momentum keep people energized and optimistic about what lies ahead.

Getting Things Moving: Taking Action

Momentum doesn't happen by chance—it starts with decisive leadership. Leaders who take action, deliver results, and make bold decisions create the conditions for forward motion. Fear and hesitation can paralyze progress, but courageous leaders push through uncertainty to get things moving.

For instance:

- In ministry: A leader might launch a new initiative or program to meet community needs, even if resources are limited.

- In business: A manager might implement a new strategy to improve sales or efficiency rather than waiting for perfect conditions.

- In education: A teacher might introduce innovative teaching methods to engage students more effectively.

Momentum begins with leaders who are willing to evaluate situations, provide solutions, and take action without fear.

Visionaries as Change Agents

Not everyone can create momentum—this is the job of visionaries. Visionary leaders see possibilities where others see obstacles. They assemble the right teams, cast compelling visions, and transmit energy through daily enthusiasm.

For example:

- In ministry: A pastor might inspire volunteers by sharing stories of lives changed through their efforts, creating excitement about future opportunities.

- In business: A CEO might rally employees around a bold vision for innovation that sparks creativity and collaboration.

- In education: A principal might unite teachers around a shared goal of improving student outcomes through teamwork and dedication.

Visionary leaders are change agents who propel momentum by inspiring others to believe in what's possible.

Passionate Leadership: Contagious Energy

Passion is one of the most powerful drivers of momentum. If you're not passionate about what you're doing, others won't be either. Passion is contagious—it ignites enthusiasm in those around you and fuels collective energy toward shared goals.

For instance:

- In ministry: A leader who speaks passionately about their faith inspires others to deepen their own spiritual journeys.

- In business: A manager who demonstrates excitement about a project encourages employees to approach their work with similar enthusiasm.

- In education: A teacher who shows genuine passion for their subject matter motivates students to engage more deeply in learning.

Passionate leaders model energy and enthusiasm that ripple throughout their organizations or communities.

Declaration and Affirmation

I declare that I am a visionary leader who creates forward motion by inspiring action and delivering results. I am a motivator who transmits passion and energy, encouraging those around me toward productivity and success.

Principle 10

The Law of Magnetic Leadership

LEADERSHIP IS ABOUT ATTRACTING the right people into your life—those who will help you grow, collaborate effectively, and achieve shared goals. Magnetic leaders cultivate qualities that draw others toward them through authenticity, positivity, and shared purpose. Who you are determines who you attract.

Attraction by Identity: Who Are You Drawing?

The people you attract into your life aren't determined by what you want—they are determined by who you are. Your character, values, and actions naturally draw like-minded individuals into your circle. To attract the right people, leaders must first look inward.

For example:

- In ministry: A pastor who models humility and servant leadership will naturally attract others who value those qualities.

- In business: A manager who prioritizes collaboration over competition will build a team that thrives on mutual respect.

- In education: A teacher who demonstrates passion for learning will inspire students who share that enthusiasm.

Magnetic leaders focus on becoming the kind of person they want to attract.

Attitude Matters: The Power of Positivity

Your attitude has a profound impact on those around you—it either draws people closer or pushes them away. Leaders who exude positivity create environments where people feel valued, motivated, and inspired to contribute.

For instance:

- In ministry: A leader with a hopeful outlook can encourage their congregation during difficult times by focusing on God's promises.

- In business: A manager who maintains optimism during challenging projects keeps morale high among their team members.

- In education: A teacher who approaches each day with enthusiasm fosters curiosity and engagement in their students.

Positive attitudes create magnetic energy that attracts others toward shared goals.

Creating Positive Environments

People gravitate toward those who make them feel good—leaders who are compassionate, kind, and uplifting naturally draw others into their orbit. Positive environments foster trust, collaboration, and growth.

For example:

- In ministry: A pastor who creates a welcoming atmosphere encourages people from all walks of life to engage with the church community.

- In business: A manager who celebrates team successes builds camaraderie among employees.

- In education: A teacher who offers encouragement rather than criticism helps students develop confidence in their abilities.

Magnetic leaders create spaces where people feel valued and empowered to thrive.

Building Commonality Across Differences

While people often connect through shared experiences or values, great leaders broaden their horizons by learning about other cultures, perspectives, and backgrounds. Respecting differences while finding common ground strengthens relationships across diverse groups.

For instance:

- In ministry: A leader might learn about cultural traditions within their congregation to foster inclusivity during worship services.

- In business: A manager might take time to understand employees' unique perspectives to build stronger team dynamics.

- In education: A teacher might incorporate diverse perspectives into lessons to help students appreciate different viewpoints.

Magnetic leaders connect authentically across differences by respecting others' values while building bridges of understanding.

Declaration and Affirmation

> *I declare that I am transformed daily into a positive being who attracts the right people into my life through authenticity and kindness.*
>
> *I am a magnet for loyalty, success, collaboration, godliness, and all that is good as I lead others toward shared goals.*

SECTION II: IMPART

PRINCIPLE THEMES:
Strategy, People Leadership, Communication, Culture

Focus Keys:
Casting vision, building teams, relational wisdom, organizational alignment

Principle 11

The Law of Genuine Connection

LEADERSHIP THRIVES ON CONNECTION. We are designed to live in community, not isolation, and leaders are called to touch people's hearts before asking for their hands. Genuine connection is the foundation of trust, collaboration, and meaningful influence. Leaders who prioritize authentic relationships inspire others to follow with loyalty and purpose.

The Heart Comes First

Great leaders understand that before you can move someone to action, you must first move their emotions. People need to feel seen, valued, and understood before they will fully commit to a vision or goal. This means prioritizing their hearts—their needs, feelings, and experiences—over their knowledge or talents.

For example:

- In ministry: A pastor who listens compassion-ately to a congregant's struggles builds trust that opens the door for spiritual guidance.

- In business: A manager who acknowledges an employee's challenges outside of work fosters loy-alty and deeper engagement.

- In education: A teacher who encourages a student struggling with self-doubt helps them build con-fidence that fuels academic success.

Leaders who connect with people emotionally create last-ing bonds that inspire action.

Self-Connectivity: Knowing Yourself First

You cannot connect with others if you are disconnected from yourself. Exceptional leaders take time for self-re-flection, developing self-awareness about their thoughts, emotions, and inner beliefs. Confidence and authenticity come from understanding who you are and embracing your strengths and growth areas.

For instance:

- In ministry: A leader who is honest about their own spiritual journey can connect more authentically with others navigating similar paths.

- In business: A manager who recognizes their leadership style and areas for improvement creates a culture of transparency and growth.

- In education: A teacher who is aware of their own biases can approach students with fairness and empathy.

Self-connected leaders lead from a place of authenticity, which strengthens their ability to connect with others meaningfully.

One Person at a Time

While leaders often address groups or audiences, true connection begins one person at a time. Exceptional leaders take the time to communicate sincerely with individuals, learning about their unique stories, needs, and aspirations. This personal touch builds trust and fosters long-term relationships.

For example:

- In ministry: A pastor might meet one-on-one with church members to understand their spiritual needs and provide tailored encouragement.

- In business: A manager might schedule regular check-ins with team members to discuss their goals and challenges.

- In education: A teacher might take time after class to help a struggling student feel supported and understood.

Leaders who focus on individuals rather than themselves create connections that go beyond surface-level interactions.

Guided Hope: Inspiring a Better Future

People look to leaders for guidance and hope—someone who can help them see beyond current challenges toward a brighter future. Exceptional leaders become "dealers of hope," encouraging others to believe in themselves and pursue their goals with optimism.

For instance:

- In ministry: A leader might remind their congregation of God's faithfulness during difficult seasons, inspiring hope for better days ahead.

- In business: A manager might motivate employees by highlighting how their work contributes to the company's long-term success.

- In education: A teacher might encourage students by showing them how hard work today will open doors for future opportunities.

Hopeful leaders inspire confidence by helping others see what's possible even in the face of obstacles.

Declaration and Affirmation

I declare that I will connect with myself and others on a genuine level, prioritizing authenticity in every interaction.

I am committed to building meaningful relationships that inspire hope, trust, and belief in the potential of those I lead.

Principle 12

The Law of Selfless Leadership

LEADERSHIP IS NOT ABOUT perks or power—it's about sacrifice. True leaders strip themselves of selfishness, putting the needs of others above their own. Sacrifice means working hard for those you lead, modeling selflessness, and investing time and effort into building something greater than yourself.

Leaders on the Frontline

Sacrifice is significant because leaders are builders—the ones responsible for laying the foundation upon which others can grow. Great leaders lead from the frontlines, modeling the work ethic they want to see in others. They put in the time, effort, and dedication necessary to inspire trust and commitment from their teams.

For example:

- In ministry: A pastor who serves alongside volunteers during outreach events demonstrates humility and dedication to the mission.

- In business: A manager who stays late to help employees meet deadlines models teamwork and commitment to excellence.

- In education: A teacher who invests extra time tutoring struggling students shows dedication to their growth and success.

Leaders on the frontline inspire others by leading through example.

The Heartbeat of Leadership

At its core, leadership is service—not status. There's a misconception that leadership is about maintaining power or enjoying privileges, but true leadership requires sacrifice for the good of others. Great leaders serve first—they are often the first ones working and the last ones to leave because they prioritize others' needs over their own.

For instance:

- In ministry: A leader might sacrifice personal time to counsel someone in need because they value people over convenience.

- In business: A CEO might forgo personal bonuses to ensure employees receive fair compensation during challenging times.

- In education: A teacher might spend evenings grading papers or preparing lessons because they care deeply about their students' success.

Selfless leaders put others first, making sacrifices that benefit those they serve.

Setting the Pace Through Sacrifice

Leaders set the pace for productivity within their organizations or teams. By sacrificing time, energy, and resources for others' progress, they establish a tone of hard work and dedication that inspires those around them.

For example:

- In ministry: A pastor who consistently shows up early for events sets an example of commitment for volunteers.

- In business: A manager who works alongside employees during busy seasons demonstrates solidarity with their team.

- In education: A principal who supports teachers during stressful periods models leadership that values people over tasks.

Pace-setting leaders inspire excellence by modeling sacrifice-driven work ethics.

The Investment Mindset

Leadership is an investment—and investments require sacrifice. Leaders invest time, energy, resources, and sometimes finances into helping others succeed. The beauty of this investment lies in seeing lives transformed as a result of your sacrifices.

For instance:

- In ministry: Mentoring young leaders may require significant time but results in a stronger future for your church or organization.

- In business: Providing training opportunities for

employees may require financial investment but leads to long-term growth.

- In education: Spending extra time preparing lessons may feel sacrificial but results in greater student engagement and achievement.

Leaders with an investment mindset understand that short-term sacrifices yield long-term rewards—for themselves *and* those they lead.

Declaration and Affirmation

I declare that I am a selfless leader who sacrifices my time, energy, and resources in service to others' growth and success.

I am an investor in people's lives, committed to building strong foundations that lead to lasting impact.

Principle 13

The Law of Dynamic Systems

LEADERSHIP THRIVES ON ORDER, clarity, and adaptability. Processes and procedures are essential for creating structure, but they must remain flexible and relevant to avoid becoming mundane or counterproductive. Leaders who prioritize well-designed systems ensure seamless integration within their teams while fostering innovation and growth.

The Importance of Process

Processes and procedures provide the framework for success. Without clear systems in place, confusion arises, productivity decreases, and momentum stalls. Leaders must establish processes that create order while empowering people to focus on their strengths.

For example:

- In ministry: A church leader might implement a clear onboarding process for new volunteers to ensure they feel equipped and welcomed into their roles.

- In business: A manager might create workflows that streamline communication across departments, reducing inefficiencies.

- In education: A principal might introduce standardized lesson-planning templates to help teachers align with curriculum goals.

Well-designed processes provide clarity, consistency, and direction for everyone involved.

Avoiding Stagnation: Keeping Systems Fresh

While processes are essential, they can become mundane or outdated if not regularly evaluated. Leaders must recognize when systems are no longer serving their purpose and adapt them to meet evolving needs. Stagnant procedures can stifle creativity and hinder progress.

For instance:

- In ministry: A leader might update outdated worship service structures to better engage a younger congregation while maintaining core values.

- In business: A manager might replace rigid reporting systems with more agile tools that allow for real-time collaboration.

- In education: A teacher might refresh classroom routines to keep students engaged and motivated throughout the school year.

Dynamic leaders ensure that processes remain relevant by regularly reviewing and refining them.

Balancing Structure with Flexibility

Effective leaders strike a balance between structure and flexibility. While processes provide stability, flexibility allows teams to adapt to new challenges or opportunities without feeling constrained by rigid systems. Leaders must empower their teams to innovate within the framework of established procedures.

For example:

- In ministry: A pastor might encourage ministry leaders to customize outreach programs based on the unique needs of their communities while adhering to overall church goals.

- In business: A CEO might allow teams to experiment with new strategies as long as they align with the company's mission and values.

- In education: A principal might give teachers autonomy in how they deliver lessons while ensuring alignment with state standards.

Flexibility within structure fosters creativity and ownership among team members.

Updating Systems for Growth

Processes should evolve alongside your organization's growth. What worked in the past may no longer be effective as your team expands or your goals shift. Leaders must proactively update systems to reflect current realities while anticipating future needs.

For instance:

- In ministry: As a church grows, a pastor might implement new communication tools or leadership structures to accommodate a larger congregation.

- In business: A manager might introduce scalable project management software as the team takes on more complex projects.

- In education: A school administrator might update professional development programs to address emerging trends in teaching methods or technology.

Leaders who embrace change ensure that their systems support growth rather than hinder it.

The Danger of No Process

Without processes in place, chaos often ensues. Teams lack direction, productivity suffers, and morale declines when people don't know what's expected of them or how to achieve success. Leaders who neglect process risk creating environments where confusion reigns.

For example:

- In ministry: Volunteers may feel overwhelmed or disengaged if there's no clear system for assigning roles or providing training.

- In business: Employees may struggle to meet deadlines if workflows are disorganized or undefined.

- In education: Students may become frustrated if classroom expectations are inconsistent or unclear.

Processes provide the foundation for order and efficiency—without them, progress becomes difficult to sustain.

Declaration and Affirmation

I declare that I will create dynamic systems that foster clarity, creativity, and growth within my organization or team.

I am committed to regularly evaluating and updating processes so they remain relevant, purposeful, and aligned with long-term success.

Principle 14

The Law of Freedom Through Forgiveness

FORGIVENESS IS A POWERFUL act that liberates both the heart and mind. Leaders who forgive lead from a place of freedom, joy, and clarity. By releasing anger, resentment, and negative thoughts, they create space for love, acceptance, and purpose. Forgiveness is not just an emotional act—it's a leadership strength that fosters connection and vision.

Renewing the Mind: Letting Go of Unforgiveness

Forgiveness begins in the mind. To lead with clarity and purpose, leaders must release unforgiving thoughts that cloud their judgment and weigh them down emotionally. A renewed mind allows leaders to focus on what truly matters—serving others and advancing their vision.

For example:

- In ministry: A pastor who forgives a congregant for harsh criticism can continue serving with an open heart rather than being distracted by bitterness.

- In business: A manager who lets go of resentment toward an employee's past mistakes can focus on mentoring them toward growth.

- In education: A teacher who forgives a student for disrespectful behavior can approach them with fresh perspective and patience.

Leaders who renew their minds through forgiveness lead with clarity, free from the burden of negativity.

Resting the Heart: Embracing Love Over Grudges

Forgiveness brings rest to the heart. When leaders let go of grudges, harsh judgments, or hatred, they create space for love, empathy, and acceptance—both for themselves and others. This emotional freedom strengthens relationships and fosters trust.

For instance:

- In ministry: A leader who forgives a team member for failing to meet expectations can rebuild trust and encourage future collaboration.

- In business: A CEO who chooses grace over anger when dealing with setbacks fosters a culture of compassion within their organization.

- In education: A principal who forgives teachers for past disagreements can work together harmoniously to improve the school environment.

A rested heart leads with love rather than resentment, creating healthier connections with others.

Restarting and Resetting: The Power of a Fresh Start

Forgiveness offers the gift of a fresh start—a reset that clears the slate of negative thoughts and emotions. Leaders who embrace this restart are better equipped to tackle challenges with renewed energy and focus. As leaders work closely with others, clashes are inevitable; forgiveness becomes essential for maintaining healthy relationships.

For example:

- In ministry: A pastor might begin each day by praying for a forgiving heart, ensuring they approach their congregation with grace.

- In business: A manager might reset their mindset after conflicts by focusing on solutions rather than dwelling on past frustrations.

- In education: A teacher might forgive themselves for mistakes in the classroom, allowing them to move forward with confidence.

A fresh start through forgiveness empowers leaders to lead without baggage or barriers.

Clarity and Purpose: Leading Without Hindrance

Forgiveness clears the path for clarity and purpose. Leaders cannot effectively cast vision or guide others if they are burdened by unresolved anger or strained relationships. By forgiving others—and themselves—leaders create space for purpose to flourish.

For instance:

- In ministry: A leader who forgives past betrayals

can focus fully on their calling without being hindered by bitterness.

- In business: A manager who reconciles with colleagues can foster collaboration that drives innovation and success.

- In education: A teacher who forgives students' missteps can inspire them toward greater effort and achievement.

Clarity born from forgiveness allows leaders to lead with focus, purpose, and authenticity.

Declaration and Affirmation

> *I declare forgiveness over my mind and heart, releasing all negative thoughts against myself or others.*
> *I am a forgiver—I choose to forgive everyone and everything so I can step into freedom, clarity, and purpose as I lead.*

Principle 15

The Law of Exponential Growth

MASSIVE GROWTH IS THE result of intentional leadership that fosters reproduction, expansion, and abundance. It works in harmony with other principles, such as attraction, abundance, and alignment. Leaders who embrace exponential growth understand the power of planning, analyzing trends, and creating environments where success multiplies.

Probability: Anticipating Outcomes

Effective leaders have a keen ability to foresee potential outcomes. This skill stems from their role as goal-setters and planners. By understanding the probability of different scenarios, leaders can guide their teams down paths that maximize success while preparing for potential challenges.

For example:

- In ministry: A pastor might anticipate how a new outreach program will impact attendance or engagement based on past efforts.

- In business: A manager might evaluate market trends to predict how a product launch will perform.

- In education: A teacher might assess how different teaching strategies will likely affect student performance.

Leaders who anticipate outcomes lead with confidence and clarity, ensuring their teams are prepared for what lies ahead.

Statistics: Measuring Productivity for Growth

Good leadership inspires productivity and results. Leaders who track these outcomes gain valuable insights into what drives success. By analyzing results, they can identify patterns, refine strategies, and make data-driven decisions that support massive growth.

For instance:

- In ministry: A church leader might track attendance or volunteer participation to understand
  what initiatives resonate most with their congregation.

- In business: A manager might analyze sales data
  to determine which products or services generate
  the most revenue.

- In education: A principal might review test scores
  to identify areas where students need additional
  support.

Leaders who use statistics effectively become strategists
who guide their teams toward greater impact.

Averages: Understanding Trends Over Time

To achieve massive growth, leaders must pay attention to
averages—the patterns that reveal when things happen,
why they occur, and how frequently they take place. By
understanding these trends, leaders can focus on what
works while eliminating what doesn't.

For example:

- In ministry: A pastor might notice that midweek services consistently have lower attendance than Sunday mornings and adjust programming accordingly.

- In business: A manager might observe that certain marketing campaigns drive higher engagement during specific seasons and allocate resources strategically.

- In education: A teacher might recognize that students perform better on assessments after interactive lessons and incorporate more hands-on activities.

By studying trends over time, leaders can make informed decisions that fuel sustained growth.

Consensus: Leveraging Popularity for Expansion

People are naturally drawn to what others are doing—growth attracts more growth. When an organization experiences momentum, it becomes magnetic, drawing others in simply because it's seen as successful or trendy. Leaders who understand what's pulling people in can amplify those efforts while refining areas that need improvement.

For instance:

- In ministry: A church experiencing growth in small groups might expand those offerings because they're fostering connection and engagement.

- In business: A company gaining traction through a popular product line might invest in scaling production to meet demand.

- In education: A school seeing increased enrollment due to innovative programs might replicate those initiatives across other grade levels.

Leaders who leverage consensus create environments where growth becomes self-sustaining.

Declaration and Affirmation

I declare that I am a leader committed to fostering exponential growth in every area of life.

I have the vision to anticipate probabilities, analyze trends, and guide others toward lasting success in business, ministry, and beyond.

Principle 16

The Law of Exemplary Leadership

CHANGE BEGINS WITH THE leader. Before guiding others toward transformation, leaders must first work on themselves. Exemplary leadership requires modeling the attitudes, behaviors, and work ethic you want to see in others. By setting the tone and leading by example, you inspire those around you to follow your lead and pursue their own growth.

Always Watching: Leading by Example

Why must change begin with you? Because as a leader, your followers are always watching. People do what you do, not what you say. Your actions carry far more weight than your words. If you want others to embrace change, hard work, or integrity, you must embody those qualities first.

For example:

- In ministry: A pastor who prioritizes prayer and personal devotion inspires their congregation to do the same.

- In business: A manager who consistently meets deadlines and works with excellence motivates their team to follow suit.

- In education: A teacher who demonstrates a love for learning encourages students to adopt a similar attitude.

Leaders who model the behavior they expect from others create a culture of accountability and authenticity.

Level Up: Let Actions Speak Louder Than Words

It's easier to tell others what to do than to model the right attitude and work ethic yourself. However, true leaders "level up" by letting their actions speak for themselves. When your followers see you practicing what you preach, they are motivated to take action and follow your example.

For instance:

- In ministry: A leader who actively participates in

community service shows their team the importance of serving others rather than just talking
about it.

- In business: A CEO who works alongside employees during busy seasons demonstrates commitment to shared goals.

- In education: A principal who engages in professional development alongside teachers models a
dedication to continuous improvement.

Actions inspire more than words ever could. Practice what
you preach, and your example will encourage others to rise
to the occasion.

Recognition: Valuing Others' Efforts

One of the most powerful tools in leadership is recognition. When people feel valued for their efforts, they become more motivated and productive. Great leaders create
cultures of recognition where individuals are celebrated
for their contributions.

For example:

- In ministry: A pastor might publicly acknowledge volunteers who go above and beyond in

serving the church community.

- In business: A manager might implement an employee recognition program that highlights achievements during team meetings.

- In education: A teacher might praise students for their hard work and progress, fostering confidence and enthusiasm.

Leadership is not about competing with others—it's about helping everyone become better versions of themselves.

Mirror Mirror: Seeking Feedback for Growth

The best leaders are self-aware and open to feedback. Sometimes we cannot see our own flaws clearly through our own lens, but by seeking input from others, we gain valuable insights into areas where we can improve. Objective feedback helps leaders transform weaknesses into strengths.

For instance:

- In ministry: A pastor might ask trusted mentors or peers for honest feedback on their preaching or leadership style.

- In business: A manager might conduct anonymous employee surveys to identify areas where they can better support their team.

- In education: A teacher might ask students or colleagues for constructive feedback on lesson delivery or classroom management.

Leaders who embrace feedback without defensiveness grow into better versions of themselves—and as they grow, they empower others to grow as well.

Declaration and Affirmation

I declare that I will strive to be better so that I can help others become better versions of themselves.
I am an agent of change who leads by example, inspires action, and fosters growth in those I serve.

Principle 17

The Law of Insightful Leadership

INSIGHTFUL LEADERSHIP IS THE ability to see beyond what is immediately visible and perceive deeper truths that guide wise decision-making. While leaders can project trends or predict outcomes, true insight allows them to anticipate challenges, navigate complexities, and lead with clarity. Leaders who cultivate insight combine wisdom, intuition, and moral integrity to guide their teams toward success.

No Formula: Principles Over Methods

There is no formula for developing insight, but there are guiding principles. Faith-based insight is rooted in God's Word and will never contradict His character. It is always moral and ethical. Leaders must use morality and values as a compass to ensure their decisions align with integrity.

For example:

- In ministry: A pastor might prayerfully consider whether a new initiative aligns with the church's mission and God's will before moving forward.

- In business: A manager might evaluate whether a decision benefits the team ethically rather than prioritizing profit alone.

- In education: A teacher might discern how to address a student's behavior by balancing fairness with compassion.

Insightful leaders measure their decisions against principles of morality, ethics, and alignment with God's truth.

Disciple Maker: Leading Through Understanding

As a leader, you are called to be a teacher—a disciple-maker who guides others toward growth and transformation. Insight helps leaders understand people's character, strengths, and learning styles so they can offer personalized guidance and advice.

For instance:

- In ministry: A leader might discern how best to

mentor someone based on their spiritual maturity and unique personality traits.

- In business: A manager might adapt their communication style to match the needs of individual team members, fostering better collaboration.

- In education: A teacher might tailor their teaching methods to suit different learning styles, ensuring all students have an opportunity to succeed.

Leaders who lead with insight build stronger relationships by understanding how to connect with those they serve effectively.

Heavenly Wisdom: Insight in Its Purest Form

True insight comes from God—it is wisdom in its purest form. Leaders who cultivate an intimate relationship with God through prayer and scripture gain access to divine understanding that surpasses human reasoning. Godly wisdom aligns with His character and provides clarity in decision-making.

For example:

- In ministry: A pastor might seek God's guidance

when navigating difficult decisions within their congregation.

- In business: A leader might pray for wisdom when faced with ethical dilemmas or high-stakes decisions.

- In education: An educator might rely on God's wisdom when addressing sensitive issues among students or colleagues.

Kingdom-minded leaders prioritize their relationship with God as the foundation for insightful leadership.

Beyond the Facts: Seeing What Others Cannot

Insight goes beyond observation or measurement—it allows leaders to perceive what others may miss. It acts as a tool for cutting through distractions, identifying the best course of action, and avoiding costly mistakes.

For instance:

- In ministry: A leader might sense underlying issues within a team that aren't immediately obvious but need addressing for unity to flourish.

- In business: A manager might recognize potential

risks in a seemingly promising opportunity and take steps to mitigate them before proceeding.

- In education: A teacher might notice hidden struggles in a student who appears fine on the surface, providing support before problems escalate.

Insight sharpens decision-making by revealing deeper truths that guide leaders toward clarity and success.

Declaration and Affirmation

I declare that I will lead with insight, making decisions that align with wisdom, morality, and God's truth.
I am a leader who possesses an insightful nature, guiding others in the right direction with clarity and integrity.

Principle 18

The Law of Multiplication Through Mentorship

TRUE LEADERSHIP IS NOT just about achieving personal success—it's about creating a legacy that outlives you. Legacy leadership focuses on equipping others to fulfill their destiny while preparing the next generation to carry the baton forward. Leaders who prioritize succession leave an enduring impact that multiplies across generations.

Legacy Living: Impact Beyond Yourself

Your leadership is meant to influence lives and inspire others to make an impact in their own spheres of influence. Leaving a legacy requires becoming your optimal self—living in alignment with your values, vision, and purpose. A legacy is not built through words alone but through consistent action that inspires others.

For example:

- In ministry: A pastor might mentor younger leaders, equipping them to serve the church long after their tenure ends.

- In business: A CEO might focus on building a company culture that empowers employees to innovate and sustain success.

- In education: A teacher might inspire students to pursue careers that will positively impact their communities.

Living a legacy means leading in a way that ensures your influence continues long after you are gone.

No One-Man Show: Raising Other Leaders

Leadership is not about you—it's about raising others. True leaders understand that success is a collective effort, not a one-man show. By empowering others to lead, you create a ripple effect that multiplies your vision and impact.

For instance:

- In ministry: A leader might delegate responsibilities to team members, allowing them to grow in their gifts while advancing the mission.

- In business: A manager might train employees to take on leadership roles, ensuring the organization thrives even in their absence.

- In education: An administrator might develop programs that empower teachers to lead initiatives within the school.

Legacy leaders focus on building teams that work together toward a shared mission and vision.

The Ripple Effect: Multiplying Your Impact

The ultimate goal of legacy leadership is to create a ripple effect—a wave of transformation that spreads far beyond your immediate circle. This requires cultivating a tribe of dedicated individuals who are committed to daily growth and self-development.

For example:

- In ministry: A pastor might encourage congregants to disciple others, creating a multiplying effect within the community.

- In business: A leader might implement mentorship programs that foster growth across all levels of the organization.

- In education: A teacher might inspire students to mentor their peers, fostering a culture of collaboration and support.

The ripple effect ensures that your influence reaches people you may never meet, creating lasting change in society.

Equip and Educate: Preparing for Succession

You cannot lead others into succession without first equipping and educating yourself. Leaders must commit to lifelong learning, gaining the knowledge and skills necessary to lead with excellence. The more you grow, the better equipped you are to empower others.

For instance:

- In ministry: A leader might attend conferences or pursue theological training to sharpen their skills for mentoring others.

- In business: A manager might invest in leadership development courses to stay ahead of industry trends and better guide their team.

- In education: A principal might seek advanced certifications or training programs to enhance their ability to support teachers effectively.

Equipped leaders create equipped teams, ensuring succession is seamless and impactful.

Declaration and Affirmation

I declare that my leadership will leave a lasting legacy, equipping others for success and preparing them for succession.

I am building a legacy that will outlast me, serving as living proof of God's presence and purpose in my life.

Principle 19

The Law of Empowered Leadership

EMPOWERED LEADERSHIP IS ABOUT raising others up—not tearing them down. True leaders celebrate the strengths of those around them rather than feeling threatened by another's success. Empowered leaders pass the baton with confidence, knowing that multiplication and growth are the ultimate goals of leadership.

Pass the Power: Multiplication Through Confidence

Many leaders feel threatened by individuals who display extraordinary skills or talents, but this insecurity stifles growth. True leaders pass the baton without fear because they understand that empowering others signals multiplication—not loss.

For example:

- In ministry: A pastor might encourage emerging leaders by giving them opportunities to preach or lead ministries within the church.

- In business: A manager might delegate key responsibilities to high-performing employees, trusting them to excel.

- In education: A teacher might encourage students with leadership potential by giving them opportunities to mentor peers or take on classroom responsibilities.

Passing power creates an environment where everyone thrives, ensuring growth for both individuals and organizations.

Know Your Worth: Celebrate Others' Light

When you know your worth as a leader, you are not threatened by someone else's success or strengths. Instead, you celebrate it and work to amplify their light so it reaches more people. Leadership is not about personal glory—it's about helping as many people as possible succeed.

For instance:

- In ministry: A leader who knows their worth will celebrate another pastor's growing influence rather than feeling envious or competitive.

- In business: A manager who values themselves will highlight an employee's achievements instead of feeling overshadowed by them.\

- In education: A teacher who is confident in their abilities will encourage colleagues' innovative ideas rather than resisting change out of insecurity.

Confident leaders inspire confidence in others, creating cultures where everyone feels valued and empowered.

Multiplication and Growth: Raising New Leaders

The ultimate goal of empowered leadership is multiplication—raising other leaders who can continue the work and expand its impact. Leaders must focus on developing others' skills so they can step into leadership roles confidently.

For example:

- In ministry: A pastor might mentor young leaders who will one day plant new churches or lead ministries independently.

- In business: A CEO might create succession plans that prepare employees for future leadership positions within the company.

- In education: An administrator might establish professional development programs that help teachers grow into instructional leaders.

Empowered leaders multiply themselves by investing in others' growth and development.

Lead Well: Love Over Fear

To lead well, you must let go of fear—fear of losing power or control—and embrace love instead. Fear leads to manipulation and insecurity, while love fosters trust, collaboration, and confidence. Leading with love means knowing who you are and leading from a place of security.

For instance:

- In ministry: A leader who leads with love will prioritize relationships over authority, building trust within their congregation or team.

- In business: A manager who leads with love will focus on collaboration rather than control, fostering innovation among employees.

- In education: A teacher who leads with love will create an environment where students feel safe to grow and succeed.

Leaders who lead well inspire loyalty and commitment from those they serve.

Declaration and Affirmation

I declare that I will lead with love, celebrating others' successes while empowering them to reach their full potential.

I am a leader who raises others up, multiplying my impact through empowered leadership rooted in confidence and compassion

Principle 20

The Law of Excellence in Details

GREAT LEADERSHIP IS FOUND in the details. Excellence is not achieved through grand gestures alone but through meticulous attention to the small things that build trust, credibility, and distinction. Leaders who focus on quality over haste create lasting impact by delivering brilliance in their work. By slowing down, concentrating on one task at a time, and valuing precision, leaders set themselves apart as extraordinary.

Meticulous Attention: Building Trust Through Precision

Attention to detail is a hallmark of reliable leadership. Leaders who are meticulous in their work inspire trust and confidence in those they lead. One small error can damage credibility, but consistent attention to detail strengthens your reputation over time.

For example:

- In ministry: A pastor who carefully prepares sermons ensures that their message is clear, impactful, and aligned with God's Word.

- In business: A manager who reviews reports thoroughly before presenting them demonstrates professionalism and reliability.

- In education: A teacher who double-checks lesson plans ensures students receive accurate and engaging instruction.

Delivering information in clear, concise, and bite-sized ways shows others that you value their time and trust.

Self-Government: Mastering Discipline for Leadership

Effective leaders practice self-government—self-discipline and self-control that guide their words, actions, and decisions. As a leader, your reputation matters. By mastering yourself, you model order, planning, and systems that inspire others to follow your example.

For instance:

- In ministry: A leader who disciplines their schedule to prioritize prayer and preparation demonstrates integrity in their calling.

- In business: A manager who organizes their tasks with precision models efficiency for their team.

- In education: A teacher who maintains consistency in classroom management creates an environment of trust and respect.

Self-governed leaders pay attention to the details of their leadership style, knowing that all eyes are on them as examples to follow.

Conservation of Detail: Setting Yourself Apart

Attention to detail is what separates ordinary leaders from stellar ones. By conserving your focus on the small but significant aspects of your work, you produce accurate results that stand out. Excellence is found in the ability to remain consistent in this zone of precision.

For example:

- In ministry: A pastor might ensure every aspect

of a worship service—music, visuals, and message—is well-coordinated for maximum impact.

- In business: A manager might oversee project timelines meticulously to ensure deadlines are met without sacrificing quality.

- In education: A teacher might pay close attention to individual student needs while maintaining overall classroom progress.

Leaders who conserve attention to detail elevate their work from average to exceptional.

Progress Over Perfection: Valuing Growth

Being attentive to detail is not about striving for perfection—it's about valuing progress. Perfection is unattainable because nothing is ever flawless; however, progress reflects growth through calculated decisions and consistent effort.

For instance:

- In ministry: A leader might celebrate small victories in church growth rather than focusing on unrealistic expectations of perfection.

- In business: A manager might recognize incremental improvements in team performance as steps toward long-term success.

- In education: A teacher might appreciate students' gradual mastery of concepts rather than expecting instant results.

Meticulous leaders value progress because it reflects intentionality and movement toward excellence without being hindered by unrealistic standards.

Declaration and Affirmation

I declare that I will be a meticulous leader who values details and progress over perfection.
I am an extraordinary leader who pays close attention to detail to produce results that inspire trust and excellence.

Principle 21

The Law of Compounding Impact

LEADERSHIP IS ABOUT INVESTING in others. The more you serve, the more you see a return—not just for yourself but for those around you. By pouring into others with humility and intention, you create a ripple effect of spiritual, emotional, and mental growth that compounds over time. True leadership multiplies impact through consistent service.

Accumulated Talents: Rising Together

Everyone has unique talents and skills. When leaders deposit their talents into helping others, they create opportunities for mutual growth. This exchange of talents nourishes both sides, fostering a community where everyone rises together. Leadership isn't about competition—it's about collaboration.

For example:

- In ministry: A pastor might mentor young leaders, equipping them to serve their congregation while learning from their fresh perspectives.

- In business: A manager might share expertise with team members while benefiting from their innovative ideas.

- In education: A teacher might guide students to discover their strengths while being inspired by their creativity and enthusiasm.

Accumulated talents build a culture of shared success where everyone contributes to collective growth.

Accumulated Influence: Impacting Lives

When leaders invest time in helping others grow, they deposit influence into their lives. This influence not only transforms those they serve but also inspires leaders to refine their own skills and character. The more you help others progress, the more your leadership influence expands.

For instance:

- In ministry: A leader who invests in discipleship programs impacts lives spiritually while deepening their own faith journey.

- In business: A manager who mentors employees sees their influence grow as team members achieve professional success.

- In education: A teacher who inspires students to pursue their potential creates a legacy of influence that extends beyond the classroom.

Influence compounds when leaders prioritize the growth and success of others.

Accumulated Credibility: Building Trust Through Service

Credibility is earned when people believe in your ability to guide them toward success. Leaders accumulate credibility by consistently helping others achieve their goals. Focus on one person at a time—small acts of service build trust that compounds over time.

For example:

- In ministry: A pastor who consistently delivers impactful sermons builds trust within their congregation.

- In business: A manager who supports employees' professional development earns loyalty and respect.

- In education: A teacher who goes the extra mile for struggling students gains credibility as a compassionate and effective educator.

Credibility grows when leaders prioritize service over self-interest.

Accumulated Blessings: Leading with Humility

Leaders are blessed when they act with humility, mercy, and faith. By becoming a blessing in others' lives, leaders open themselves up to receive blessings in return. True leadership is rooted in a forgiving nature, pure intentions, and a desire to serve selflessly.

For instance:

- In ministry: A leader who serves with humility

inspires others to live out their faith authentically.

- In business: A manager who leads with compassion creates an environment where employees feel valued and supported.

- In education: A teacher who approaches students with patience and understanding fosters trust and respect.

Blessings accumulate when leaders focus on serving others with love and humility.

Declaration and Affirmation

I declare that every step I take is intentional and designed to help others grow and succeed.

I am a leader who invests my time, talents, and skills into creating lasting impact in the lives of those I serve.

SECTION III: RELEASE

PRINCIPLE THEMES:
Legacy, Succession, Expansion, Spiritual Authority

Focus Keys:

Releasing others, stewarding platforms, apostolic vision, eternal impact

Principle 22

The Law of Unified Triumph

TRUE LEADERSHIP IS MEASURED by collective success, not individual wins. Leaders pursue victory for their entire team, ensuring that everyone rises together. Unified triumph is achieved through perseverance, responsibility, and the ability to embrace diversity while fostering unity.

Leaders Find a Way: Winning Together

It's not a win if the team isn't winning together. Great leaders focus on finding solutions that benefit everyone involved. They don't fold under pressure but instead find ways around obstacles or through them, inspiring their teams to do the same.

For example:

- In ministry: A pastor might rally volunteers to

overcome challenges during an outreach event by focusing on shared goals rather than setbacks.

- In business: A manager might lead brainstorming sessions to find creative solutions to meet deadlines without sacrificing quality.

- In education: A teacher might adapt lesson plans to ensure all students grasp key concepts despite varying learning styles.

Leaders find ways for the team to win collectively because success is always shared.

Leading Responsibly: Setting the Tone

Leaders recognize that they are responsible for setting the tone for creativity, empowerment, commitment, and results within their teams or organizations. Leadership starts at the top—it trickles down from how leaders model behavior to how teams operate daily.

For instance:

- In ministry: A leader who models dedication inspires volunteers to commit wholeheartedly to the mission.

- In business: A CEO who fosters innovation encourages employees to think outside the box while staying aligned with company values.

- In education: A principal who demonstrates accountability motivates teachers to uphold high standards in their classrooms.

Responsible leadership creates environments where teams thrive under clear direction and purpose.

Quitting Is Not an Option: Overcoming Obstacles

Extraordinary leaders refuse to surrender to challenges—they are natural overcomers who face obstacles with courage and determination. They don't accept "no" as an answer but instead choose perseverance over fear.

For example:

- In ministry: A pastor might persist in building community programs despite limited resources or initial setbacks.

- In business: A manager might encourage their team to keep pushing forward after failed attempts at launching a product or service.

- In education: A teacher might work tirelessly with struggling students until they achieve break-throughs in understanding.

Leaders inspire perseverance by modeling resilience in the face of adversity.

Unity Through Diversity: Strength in Differences

The best leaders embrace diversity as a strength rather than a challenge. They identify individual strengths within their teams and unite them toward shared goals while turning weaknesses into opportunities for growth.

For instance:

- In ministry: A leader might bring together people from different backgrounds to create inclusive worship experiences that reflect unity in Christ.

- In business: A manager might leverage diverse perspectives within a team to drive innovation and creativity in problem-solving.

- In education: A teacher might celebrate cultural differences among students while fostering collaboration in group projects.

Unity through diversity creates stronger teams capable of achieving greater triumphs together.

Declaration and Affirmation

I declare that I will unite my team by embracing differences and fostering collaboration toward shared victories.

I am a leader who never quits, inspiring perseverance and triumph in myself and those I serve.

Principle 23

The Law of Purposeful Priorities

GREAT LEADERS UNDERSTAND THAT success is built on purposeful prioritization. They identify what matters most and organize their efforts to align with the organization's goals and vision. By focusing on what truly matters, leaders create clarity, direction, and momentum for their teams.

Large-Scale Leadership: Vision Shapes Priorities

Do you have a global vision or a small-scale focus? Stellar leaders make decisions based on priorities that align with their long-term vision. They recognize that not all tasks carry equal weight—some have a greater impact and must take precedence.

For example:

- In ministry: A pastor might prioritize discipleship programs that foster spiritual growth over events that only provide short-term engagement.

- In business: A manager might focus on high-impact projects that drive revenue rather than getting bogged down in minor administrative tasks.

- In education: A principal might prioritize initiatives that improve student outcomes over less critical activities.

Leaders with a clear vision set priorities that drive meaningful progress toward their goals.

Communicating Priorities: Directing with Purpose

Clear communication is essential for establishing priorities. Leaders must articulate their vision and purpose-based priorities to their teams, providing a clear path forward. When leaders communicate effectively, they become a compass, guiding others to take purposeful steps.

For instance:

- In ministry: A leader might hold regular meetings

to communicate the church's mission and how each program aligns with it.

- In business: A manager might use team briefings to clarify project goals and ensure everyone understands their role.

- In education: A teacher might explain how each lesson connects to broader learning objectives, helping students stay focused.

Purposeful communication ensures everyone is aligned and working toward shared priorities.

Connection: Leading Through Care

Leaders cannot accomplish anything without first connecting with their people. Emotional bonds are the foundation of trust and collaboration. When people feel valued and cared for, they are more likely to follow your lead and commit to shared priorities.

For example:

- In ministry: A pastor who takes time to listen to congregants' concerns fosters trust that strengthens the church community.

- In business: A manager who builds rapport with employees creates a culture where team members feel motivated to contribute.

- In education: A teacher who connects with students on a personal level inspires them to engage more deeply in learning.

Leaders who prioritize connection build teams that are unified in purpose.

Innovation: Prioritizing for Maximum Impact

Successful leaders live by purposeful priorities—they focus on what yields the greatest return and reward for everyone involved. By identifying high-impact tasks, they maximize productivity and innovation while avoiding distractions.

For instance:

- In ministry: A leader might prioritize outreach programs that meet pressing community needs while fostering spiritual growth.

- In business: A CEO might focus on developing products or services that deliver long-term value rather than chasing short-term trends.

- In education: An administrator might prioritize professional development opportunities that enhance teaching effectiveness across the school.

Prioritizing for maximum impact ensures progress is both meaningful and sustainable.

Declaration and Affirmation

> *I declare that every step I take is intentional, leading me to identify purposeful priorities for success.*
>
> *I am a leader who prioritizes according to what brings the greatest rewards for my team and those I serve.*

Principle 24

The Law of Accountable Leadership

OUTSTANDING LEADERS ARE TRUSTWORTHY because they hold themselves accountable first. Accountability begins with self-discipline, maturity, confidence, preparation, and experience. Leaders who embrace accountability inspire trust, respect, and loyalty from those they lead.

Maturity: The Foundation of Accountability

Mature leaders possess the right motives—they act with wisdom and integrity rather than impulsiveness or self-interest. Maturity allows leaders to analyze situations thoroughly before making decisions, ensuring their timing and actions align with purpose.

For example:

- In ministry: A pastor might seek counsel from

trusted mentors before making major decisions affecting the congregation.

- In business: A manager might evaluate all available data before implementing changes to ensure they benefit the team.

- In education: A teacher might reflect on feedback from students or colleagues to refine their teaching methods.

Maturity is cultivated through understanding, feedback, and thoughtful decision-making.

Confidence: Inspiring Trust Through Stability

People follow leaders who exude confidence—those who know where they're headed and believe in their vision. Confidence provides stability in leadership; no one will follow someone who appears uncertain or unstable.

For instance:

- In ministry: A leader who confidently casts vision inspires congregants to rally behind shared goals.

- In business: A manager who approaches challenges with assurance motivates employees to persevere through obstacles.

- In education: A principal who confidently implements new policies earns trust from teachers, students, and parents alike.

Confident leaders inspire others to believe in their direction and abilities.

Preparation: Planning for Success

Accountable leaders don't leave success up to chance—they prepare thoroughly and execute their plans with precision. The wrong action at the right time can lead to mistakes; preparation ensures actions align with purpose.

For example:

- In ministry: A pastor who prepares sermons thoughtfully delivers messages that resonate deeply with their congregation.

- In business: A manager who plans meetings effectively ensures productive discussions that drive results.

- In education: A teacher who prepares lessons

carefully creates engaging experiences that enhance student learning.

Preparation is the bridge between intention and execution
in leadership.

Experience: Growing Through Challenges

Experience is one of the greatest teachers in leadership—it
provides wisdom that cannot be gained any other way.
Leaders grow by saying "yes" to opportunities that challenge them outside their comfort zones, cultivating skills
through real-world application.

For instance:

- In ministry: A leader might take on new responsibilities within their church to gain experience in
  different areas of service.

- In business: An entrepreneur might embrace risks
  associated with launching new ventures as opportunities for growth.

- In education: An educator might pursue leadership roles within their school district to expand
  their influence.

Leaders gain credibility through experience, which equips them to guide others effectively.

Declaration and Affirmation

I declare that I possess wisdom, maturity, confidence, preparation, and experience as a leader.

I am an accountable leader who provides guidance rooted in trustworthiness and intentionality.

Principle 25

The Law of Creative Leadership

CREATIVITY IS AT THE heart of innovation, and every leader has the responsibility to unleash the creative potential within their team. Leaders who foster creativity empower their people to think boldly, act decisively, and embrace their strengths. By cultivating an environment that inspires innovation, leaders pave the way for transformative results.

Everything Falls on Leadership: Empowering Creativity

If your team isn't unlocking their creativity, it's a reflection of leadership. Leaders are the motivators of creativity—they set the tone for empowerment and innovation. A true leader develops other leaders by giving them autonomy to make decisions and take ownership of their work. When people feel empowered, they naturally become more innovative.

For example:

- In ministry: A pastor might encourage ministry leaders to design new outreach programs tailored to their community's needs.

- In business: A manager might allow team members to experiment with creative solutions to solve challenges.

- In education: A teacher might give students freedom to approach projects in unique ways that reflect their individual strengths.

Empowered teams thrive in creativity because they feel trusted and valued.

Leaders Develop Leaders: Building Self-Mastery

The best leaders don't just lead—they develop other leaders. This begins by helping people discover themselves and encouraging them to master their own strengths. Self-mastery is the foundation for confident, creative leadership.

For instance:

- In ministry: A leader might mentor others by helping them identify their spiritual gifts and how to use them effectively.

- In business: A manager might guide employees in setting personal development goals that align with company objectives.

- In education: A teacher might encourage students to reflect on their learning styles and how they can apply them to solve problems creatively.

Leaders who build self-mastery in others create a ripple effect of innovation and growth.

Challenge and Small Wins: Building Confidence

Confidence is key to unlocking creativity. Leaders can help their teams embrace their potential by challenging them to step out of their comfort zones. Small wins along the way build momentum and reinforce confidence in their abilities.

For example:

- In ministry: A pastor might challenge a young

leader to deliver a sermon or lead a small group for the first time.

- In business: A manager might assign a high-potential employee a stretch project that pushes them beyond their usual responsibilities.

- In education: A teacher might encourage students to tackle complex problems incrementally, celebrating each milestone achieved.

Small wins inspire big breakthroughs by showing people what they're capable of achieving.

Culture and Conditioning: Creating Space for Innovation

As a leader, you shape the culture within your organization or team. Your culture will either inspire innovation or stifle it with fear. Create an environment where out-of-the-box thinking is encouraged, and no idea is dismissed as "too crazy." One idea often leads to another—and eventually, the breakthrough that drives transformative results.

For instance:

- In ministry: A leader might host brainstorming

sessions where all ideas are welcomed without judgment.

- In business: A manager might create open forums where employees can pitch creative solutions or new product ideas.

- In education: A teacher might foster classroom discussions where students are encouraged to share unconventional approaches.

Innovative cultures thrive when people feel safe to explore bold ideas without fear of failure or criticism.

Declaration and Affirmation

> *I declare that I will empower others to think boldly, act creatively, and embrace autonomy in their work.*
> *I am a leader who fosters innovation by encouraging outrageous thinking and cultivating an environment where ideas flourish.*

Principle 26

The Law of Visionary Execution

Visionary leaders don't just talk about ideas—they bring them to life through precise articulation, strategic planning, and relentless execution. Transmitting vision effectively requires clarity, action, and unwavering commitment. Leaders who execute well inspire loyalty, unity, and productivity within their teams.

Execution Is Key: Turning Vision Into Action

A vision without execution is just words. Great leaders establish clear plans for bringing their vision to life—and then follow through with decisive action. Words alone cannot inspire change; action is what makes vision tangible.

For example:

- In ministry: A pastor might outline actionable steps for launching a new community outreach program while rallying volunteers to execute it effectively.

- In business: A CEO might create a roadmap for achieving company goals while ensuring every department understands its role in execution.

- In education: An administrator might implement strategies for improving student outcomes while tracking progress over time.

Execution transforms vision into reality by turning ideas into measurable results.

Relentless Drive: Staying Committed

Visionary leaders demonstrate relentless drive—they don't falter or lose focus when challenges arise. Their passion fuels their perseverance, inspiring those around them to stay committed until the vision is fully realized.

For instance:

- In ministry: A leader might push forward with

faith during difficult seasons, trusting that God's plan will come to fruition.

- In business: A manager might maintain enthusiasm during setbacks, motivating employees to keep striving toward success.

- In education: A teacher might remain dedicated despite obstacles, ensuring students stay engaged in learning.

Relentless drive inspires teams to persevere through challenges with confidence and determination.

Zero Division: Inspiring Unity Through Vision

When leaders transmit their vision with clarity and accuracy, they inspire unity among their teams or organizations. Division has no room in environments where everyone feels valued and involved in achieving shared goals.

For example:

- In ministry: A pastor who communicates vision clearly fosters alignment among church staff and volunteers.

- In business: A manager who involves employees

in decision-making builds loyalty and collaboration within the team.

- In education: An administrator who listens to teachers' input creates a unified approach to improving school performance.

Unity strengthens teams by ensuring everyone works together toward a common purpose.

Reach Without Limits: Inspiring Growth

Visionary leaders challenge their teams to reach beyond perceived limitations while making them feel valued and appreciated along the way. They set high expectations but provide encouragement that inspires confidence and productivity.

For instance:

- In ministry: A leader might encourage members of their congregation to take on leadership roles they never thought possible.

- In business: A manager might challenge employees to exceed performance benchmarks while recognizing their contributions regularly.

- In education: A teacher might push students toward academic excellence while celebrating individual progress milestones.

Leaders who inspire growth create environments where people feel empowered to achieve more than they ever imagined possible.

Declaration and Affirmation

I declare that I will transmit my vision with clarity, purpose, and actionable steps that inspire unity and productivity among my team.

I am a visionary leader who executes plans relentlessly while fostering an environment of growth and improvement.

Principle 27

The Law of Empowered Belief

BELIEF IS THE FOUNDATION of success. Without belief in yourself and your team, progress is impossible. Leaders who cultivate belief inspire confidence, courage, and optimism in themselves and those they lead. Empowered belief is the driving force behind bold action, resilience, and achievement.

Change Your Self-Talk: Rewriting Your Inner Narrative

Belief begins with how you speak to yourself. Negative self-talk creates doubt, while positive affirmations build confidence. To create a new set of beliefs, replace negative words with empowering ones. Make this a daily habit, and over time, it will become part of your lifestyle.

For example:

- In ministry: A pastor might remind themselves daily of God's promises to overcome feelings of inadequacy in their calling.

- In business: A manager might affirm their ability to lead effectively before tackling challenging projects.

- In education: A teacher might replace thoughts of frustration with affirmations about their ability to inspire students.

Changing your self-talk transforms doubt into belief, setting the stage for success.

Commit to Courage: Learning Through Action

Belief grows when you commit to courage—making decisions and taking responsibility for the outcomes, whether good or bad. Success doesn't come from avoiding mistakes; it comes from learning through them. Courageous leaders embrace failure as part of the journey.

For instance:

- In ministry: A leader might take a bold step to

launch a new program, trusting God's guidance even if challenges arise.

- In business: An entrepreneur might commit to launching a product despite uncertainty about market reception.

- In education: A teacher might try innovative teaching methods, knowing there's always room for adjustment.

Courage builds belief by showing you that mistakes are stepping stones to growth.

Take Risks: Boldness Inspires Others

Belief is strengthened when you take risks and step out of your comfort zone. Even if you fail, people will admire your boldness because it reflects strength they wish they had themselves. Risk-takers inspire others by demonstrating what's possible when fear doesn't hold them back.

For example:

- In ministry: A pastor might take a risk by addressing sensitive topics that need to be discussed within their congregation.

- In business: A manager might pursue an unconventional strategy that could yield transformative results.

- In education: A teacher might introduce creative projects that challenge students to think outside the box.

Taking risks not only builds your own belief but also inspires those around you to be fearless.

Optimism Breeds Belief: Becoming a Magnet for Positivity

Optimism is a powerful force that fuels belief. When you choose to focus on the good, you naturally attract positivity and inspire others to do the same. Optimism helps you avoid negative thought patterns and reinforces confidence in yourself and your abilities.

For instance:

- In ministry: A leader who remains optimistic during tough seasons encourages their congregation to trust in God's plan.

- In business: A manager who maintains a positive outlook during challenges motivates their team to stay focused on solutions.

- In education: A teacher who celebrates small victories inspires students to believe in their potential.

Optimism creates an environment where belief flourishes, both within yourself and among those you lead.

Declaration and Affirmation

I declare that I will strengthen my belief in myself and inspire others to believe in themselves as well.
I am a confident leader who embraces courage, takes risks, and fosters optimism in every situation.

Principle 28

The Law of Courageous Communication

LEADERSHIP BEGINS WITH LISTENING. When leaders actively listen to those they serve, they build trust, loyalty, and meaningful connections. Intentional listening is an investment in people—it shows them they are valued and creates a foundation for collaboration and growth.

Listening Is an Investment: Valuing Time with Others

Time is one of the most valuable resources you can give someone because it can never be reclaimed. When you choose to listen attentively, you are investing in their growth, concerns, or ideas. This investment often yields significant returns as people feel valued and empowered.

For example:

- In ministry: A pastor who listens attentively during counseling sessions builds trust with their congregation.

- In business: A manager who takes time to hear employees' feedback fosters loyalty and engagement within the team.

- In education: A teacher who listens carefully to students' struggles creates a safe space for learning and growth.

Listening is an act of service that strengthens relationships while building trust.

Fairness: Treating People with Understanding

Fairness is about treating people with respect and understanding their unique perspectives or needs. Leaders who are fair create environments where everyone feels valued and appreciated for who they are.

For instance:

- In ministry: A leader who treats volunteers fairly ensures everyone feels equally important in advancing the mission.

- In business: A manager who considers diverse viewpoints when making decisions fosters inclusivity within the workplace.

- In education: A teacher who adapts lessons for students with different learning styles demonstrates fairness in meeting individual needs.

Fairness builds trust by showing people they are seen, heard, and respected.

Manifest Loyalty: Inspiring Trust Through Listening

When people feel heard, they develop loyalty toward their leader because they know their voice matters. Leaders who listen attentively inspire respect and trust—two essential components of strong relationships.

For example:

- In ministry: A pastor who listens deeply to congregants' concerns inspires loyalty within their church community.

- In business: A manager who addresses employees'

feedback thoughtfully earns respect from their team members.

- In education: A teacher who listens empathetically to students' struggles fosters trust that enhances classroom dynamics.

Loyalty is cultivated when leaders genuinely care about what others have to say.

Honoring Trust: Building Reciprocal Relationships

Trust is the cornerstone of leadership—it must be built daily through consistent communication, integrity, and responsibility. Leaders who honor trust create two-way relationships where respect is reciprocated, fostering collaboration and mutual growth.

For instance:

- In ministry: A leader who keeps their word strengthens trust within their congregation or team.

- In business: A manager who follows through on promises builds credibility among employees.

- In education: A teacher who consistently shows

up for students earns their trust over time.

True leadership is measured by moments where trust is honored through action.

Declaration and Affirmation

> *I declare that I will listen intentionally, treating others with fairness while building trust through my actions. I am a loyal leader who values others deeply and invests in them because I see their worth.*

Principle 29

The Law of Mutual Growth

GREAT LEADERS UNDERSTAND THAT growth is a collaborative process. Just as iron sharpens iron, leaders use every moment as an opportunity to teach, guide, and help others grow. By fostering environments where strengths are refined and weaknesses are addressed, leaders ensure that everyone becomes sharper, stronger, and more effective.

Problem Solving: Focusing on Solutions

Leaders don't dwell on problems—they pivot toward solutions. They welcome advice, opinions, and collaboration to ensure challenges are addressed effectively. Problem-solving is a team effort, and great leaders create spaces where everyone's input is valued.

For example:

- In ministry: A pastor might gather their leadership team to brainstorm solutions for increasing community engagement.

- In business: A manager might hold collaborative sessions to address workflow inefficiencies and implement improvements.

- In education: A teacher might involve students in finding creative ways to overcome classroom challenges.

Leaders who focus on solutions inspire their teams to approach problems with confidence and creativity.

Sharp Blades: The Power of Collaboration

When two iron edges rub together, both become sharper. Similarly, when people work together, they refine each other's strengths. Collaboration creates mutual advantage—sharper skills, better ideas, and greater effectiveness.

For instance:

- In ministry: A pastor might pair experienced leaders with newer ones to mentor them while learning fresh perspectives in return.

- In business: A manager might create cross-functional teams where employees from different departments sharpen each other's expertise.

- In education: A teacher might encourage peer-to-peer learning where students challenge and support one another.

Collaboration ensures that everyone grows stronger together.

Working Toward Greatness: Sharpening Others' Strengths

Great leaders are committed to helping others evolve into their optimal selves. By sharpening the strengths and abilities of those they lead, they create a collective path toward greatness. Leadership isn't just about personal success—it's about elevating others.

For example:

- In ministry: A leader might invest time in developing the spiritual gifts of their congregation members.

- In business: A manager might provide training opportunities to help employees enhance their skills.

- In education: A teacher might encourage students to pursue their passions while guiding them toward academic excellence.

Leaders achieve greatness by helping others reach their full potential.

Team-Building: Growing Together

Leaders understand that growth happens when people come together to pursue shared goals. By uniting efforts and strengths, they create teams that sharpen each other through collaboration and mutual support. Organizations experience the most growth when individuals work together toward a common purpose.

For instance:

- In ministry: A pastor might organize team-building retreats to strengthen relationships among church staff and volunteers.

- In business: A manager might foster collaboration through group projects that leverage diverse talents.

- In education: A teacher might assign coopera-
  tive learning activities that encourage students to
  work together effectively.

Team-building fosters growth by creating environments
where people learn from and support one another.

Declaration and Affirmation

> *I declare that I will build up others by fostering connec-
> tions, collaboration, and mutual growth. I am a leader
> who sharpens strengths and unites teams to achieve
> greatness together.*

Principle 30

The Law of Authentic Acceptance

ACCEPTANCE IS THE FOUNDATION of authentic leadership. It begins with letting go of control—not attaching yourself to people or outcomes but instead focusing on the vision. Leaders who embrace acceptance foster self-awareness in themselves and others while creating environments of trust and positivity.

Acceptance of Ourselves: Embracing Truth for Growth

Self-awareness is the first step toward acceptance. Leaders must recognize their strengths, flaws, and current reality before they can grow or lead effectively. Acceptance doesn't mean settling—it means acknowledging where you are so you can move forward with purpose.

For example:

☐   In ministry: A pastor might reflect on areas where they need spiritual growth while celebrating the progress they've made in their calling.

☐   In business: A leader might acknowledge gaps in their skills while committing to personal development through training or mentorship.

☐   In education: A teacher might recognize areas for improvement in classroom management while building on their teaching strengths.

Acceptance of yourself creates a foundation for meaningful change.

Acceptance of Others: Leading Without Judgment

Accepting others doesn't mean agreeing with everything they say or do—it means recognizing their humanity and meeting them where they are. Great leaders guide others toward self-awareness without confrontation or judgment, inspiring growth through encouragement rather than criticism.

For instance:

☐   In ministry: A pastor might mentor someone struggling with faith by listening empathetically rather than imposing solutions.

☐   In business: A manager might support an employee's professional development by understanding their unique challenges and goals.

☐   In education: A teacher might work patiently with students who learn differently, helping them find strategies that work for them.

Acceptance builds trust by showing people they are valued as individuals.

Moving Forward: Acceptance as a Catalyst for Progress

Acceptance doesn't mean staying stagnant—it's about understanding what needs to change so you can move forward boldly. Leaders who embrace acceptance make tough decisions with clarity because they've acknowledged reality without resistance.

For example:

☐   In ministry: A leader might accept that certain programs aren't working and pivot to new strategies that better serve their community.

☐   In business: A manager might recognize market shifts and adapt company goals accordingly rather than clinging to outdated plans.

☐   In education: An educator might adjust teaching methods based on student feedback to improve learning outcomes.

Acceptance paves the way for progress by removing resistance to change.

Environment of Acceptance: Leading with Humanity

The best leaders create environments where people feel accepted as they are—not judged or treated as mere tools for productivity. They acknowledge people's humanity by fostering positivity, trust, and mutual respect within their teams or organizations.

For instance:

□   In ministry: A pastor might create a welcoming church culture where everyone feels valued regardless of background or struggles.

□   In business: A leader might cultivate an inclusive workplace where employees feel safe sharing ideas without fear of judgment.

□   In education: A teacher might foster a classroom environment where students feel supported in expressing themselves authentically.

Environments of acceptance inspire loyalty, trust, and collaboration among those you lead.

Declaration and Affirmation

> *I declare that I will accept myself fully while guiding others toward self-awareness and purpose-driven growth.*
>
> *I am a leader who fosters trust through acceptance, creating environments where everyone feels valued and inspired to succeed.*

Principle 31

The Law of Empowering Embrace

THE GREATEST GIFT A leader can give is to embrace people as they are while empowering them to grow into their best selves. Leaders who practice the art of embracing foster environments where individuals feel valued, accepted, and inspired to contribute fully. Embracing others builds trust, authenticity, and unity within teams.

Embracing New Ideas: Building Belief Through Validation

People are often accustomed to rejection or dismissal, which makes it powerful when a leader validates their perspectives and ideas. By embracing new ideas, leaders build belief in others and guide them toward refining their thoughts into actionable solutions.

For example:

☐   In ministry: A pastor might encourage volunteers to share creative ideas for outreach programs and work with them to bring those ideas to life.

☐   In business: A manager might validate an employee's innovative proposal by providing resources to test its feasibility.

☐   In education: A teacher might embrace a student's unconventional approach to solving a problem, guiding them to develop their critical thinking skills.

Leaders who embrace new ideas inspire confidence and creativity in those they lead.

Embrace Your Team: Empowering Collective Strength

Your team is the driving force behind the vision and mission. Embracing your team means empowering them to work harder, collaborate effectively, and bring goals to life in real-time. When leaders embrace their teams, they create unity and momentum.

For instance:

☐   In ministry: A pastor might empower church staff by delegating responsibilities that align with their strengths and passions.

☐   In business: A manager might foster teamwork by encouraging collaboration on high-impact projects that require diverse skill sets.

☐   In education: A principal might empower teachers by providing autonomy in how they deliver lessons while offering support when needed.

Empowered teams achieve more because they feel trusted and valued.

Embracing Authenticity: Encouraging People to Be Themselves

Authenticity is one of the most valuable traits within a team. Leaders who embrace authenticity encourage people to be themselves without fear of judgment or rejection. By celebrating differences, leaders create environments where individuals feel free to contribute their unique perspectives.

For example:

☐   In ministry: A leader might celebrate the diverse spiritual gifts within their congregation, encouraging members to use them for collective growth.

☐   In business: A manager might foster an inclusive culture where employees feel safe expressing their ideas and individuality.

☐   In education: A teacher might encourage students to explore their unique talents and interests as part of their learning journey.

Authenticity strengthens teams by allowing everyone to bring their full selves to the table.

Embrace Inclusivity: Learning from Diversity

Inclusivity is essential for building strong connections within teams. Leaders who embrace inclusivity seek to understand different cultures, perspectives, and experiences. By learning from others, leaders create bonds that strengthen collaboration and foster success.

For instance:

☐   In ministry: A pastor might incorporate diverse cultural traditions into worship services to create a more inclusive community.

☐   In business: A leader might actively seek input from team members with diverse backgrounds to ensure all voices are heard.

☐   In education: An educator might design lesson plans that celebrate cultural diversity while promoting mutual respect among students.

Inclusivity fosters unity by ensuring everyone feels seen, heard, and valued.

Declaration and Affirmation

> *I declare that I will lead with inclusivity, acceptance, and empowerment for myself and those I serve.*
> *I am a leader who embraces others fully while inspiring them to grow into their best selves through authenticity and collaboration.*

LEARN, APPLY, AND MULTIPLY

LEADERSHIP IS ABOUT LEGACY—ABOUT passing the baton to the next generation and leaving an impact that outlives you. The goal is to lead from a healthy place spiritually, mentally, and emotionally. Without this foundation, you risk hurting others in the process.

Leadership is not just about what you accomplish but about how you empower others to grow and succeed.

We all have unique strengths, skills, and talents that are meant to be shared for the advancement of others. In leadership, these strengths are your greatest assets. Take a moment to reflect: What are your internal assets? What makes you a valuable leader? Why should others follow your lead, and what are you bringing to the table?

Your greatest assets are not just your abilities but also your willingness to use them to help others. Ask yourself: How can I improve someone else's life today? Deep within you lies wisdom gained from your experiences—wisdom waiting to be released. People need to hear your story, your struggles, and how you overcame obstacles because your journey might hold the key to unlocking someone else's potential. Your formula for overcoming challenges could be the breakthrough someone else desperately needs.

Transform Yourself First

Before you can positively impact others, you must first work on yourself. Leadership begins with inner transformation—building confidence, healing from past wounds, and trusting in your abilities. Confidence stems from belief in yourself, but flawed or distorted belief systems can cloud your judgment and actions. You must clear the fog by addressing limiting beliefs and viewing yourself through a lens of truth and positivity.

When you heal and grow, you lead from a place of authenticity and strength. This self-transformation allows you to guide others with clarity, purpose, and compassion.

Vision Creates Momentum

Leaders are visionaries who inspire momentum through enthusiasm and confidence. Are you a visionary? Can you gather the right people around a shared goal? Visionary leaders motivate others to take action and embark on their own transformational journeys. Think about how you are currently inspiring those around you: Are you transmitting passion? Are you encouraging growth?

Momentum begins with passion—it's contagious. When you lead with passion, it ignites excitement in others and propels them forward toward achieving shared goals.

Leadership Is Service

At its core, leadership is about serving others. True leaders sacrifice personal interests for the benefit of their team or organization. Leadership is not about power or perks—it's about humility, selflessness, and hard work. The best leaders serve the most; they are the first to step in and the last to leave. They set the tone for productivity, commitment, and excellence through their actions.

Serving as a leader requires sacrifice—it's a sacrificial act of love for those you lead. It means putting yourself last so that others can rise. It means being willing to uplift, encourage, guide, and equip people to become their best selves so they can help others do the same.

A Call to Authentic Leadership

Leadership is not about perfection; it's about authenticity. We all have an audience we are meant to reach—a unique group of people who need what only we can offer. Embrace both your strengths and weaknesses as part of your leadership journey. View your weaknesses as opportunities for collaboration—a chance to connect with others in meaningful ways that highlight our shared humanity.

Right now, I challenge you to embrace every season of your leadership journey—the victories, the challenges, and everything in between. Think deeply about your purpose as a leader. Evaluate where you are now and where you want to go. Commit yourself to continuous learning and growth so that you can equip others with the knowledge they need to succeed.

Release what you've learned onto others with humility and grace. Be authentic in all that you do—because authenticity builds trust, fosters connection, and creates lasting impact.

Building a Legacy That Lasts

Leadership is not just about what happens today—it's about creating a legacy that will inspire future generations. As a leader, your priority is not only achieving goals but also raising up others who will carry on the mission long after you're gone. By embracing this responsibility with humility and purpose, you will leave behind something far greater than accomplishments—you will leave behind transformed lives.

So embrace this journey wholeheartedly. Lead with passion, serve selflessly, inspire boldly, and build connections rooted in trust and authenticity. Learn relentlessly, apply what you've learned with intention, and multiply that knowledge by empowering others.

This is how legacies are built—through service, authenticity, growth, and love for those we lead. Step into your leadership role with confidence and joy as you work toward building something extraordinary that will outlast us all.

Let's go change lives—starting today!

www.ingramcontent.com/pod-product-compliance
Lightning Source LLC
Chambersburg PA
CBHW071438090426
42737CB00011B/1706